LETTRES ACADIENNES
A Cajun ABC

Written and Illustrated by
DON GOODRUM

PELICAN PUBLISHING COMPANY
Gretna 1992

*The word "Pelican" and the depiction of a pelican are trademarks
of Pelican Publishing Company, Inc., and are registered in the
U.S. Patent and Trademark Office.*

Library of Congress Cataloging-in-Publication Data

Goodrum, Don.
    Lettres acadiennes : a Cajun ABC / written and illustrated by Don
Goodrum.
        p.   cm.
    Summary: An alphabetical introduction to Cajun vocabulary and
culture.
    ISBN 0-88289-899-X
    1. Cajun French dialect--Alphabet--Juvenile literature.
2. Cajuns--Louisiana--Juvenile literature. [1. Cajun French
dialect. 2. Cajuns. 3. Alphabet.] I. Title.
PC3680.U7L7362 1992
447'.9763--dc20
[E]   92-5124
                                                          CIP
                                                          AC

*This is for my darling daughters, Sara, Blayre, and Brittany, without
whom none of this would have ever gotten started, and for my wife, Brenda,
who always believed . . . even when I didn't.*

Special thanks go to Diane McDermott for the idea and cheerleading in
general, and to Glen Pitre and Michelle Benoit for knowing the right people
and graciously introducing me to them, for taking the time to help me
with all the French, and most of all for sharing with me their love for
Louisiana. Also thanks to my parents for letting me be myself and to my
editor, Nina Kooij, Dana Bilbray and all the folks at Pelican for taking
a chance. And finally, to anyone who ever patted me on the back and said,
"Don't give up!" — this one's for you. Thanks.

Manufactured in Hong Kong

Published by Pelican Publishing Company, Inc.
1101 Monroe Street, Gretna, Louisiana 70053

ALPHONSE, the ARDENT ARMADILLO ALWAYS ANSWERS AVEC AMOUR

ACADIA

ALPHABET
Aa Bb Cc Dd
Ff Gg Hh
Kk Ll M... Oo
Pp Rr Ss Tt

ATCHAFALAYA BAND

AMBULANCE

the AMAZING ANDOUILLE FESTIVAL

LaPlace, Louisiana

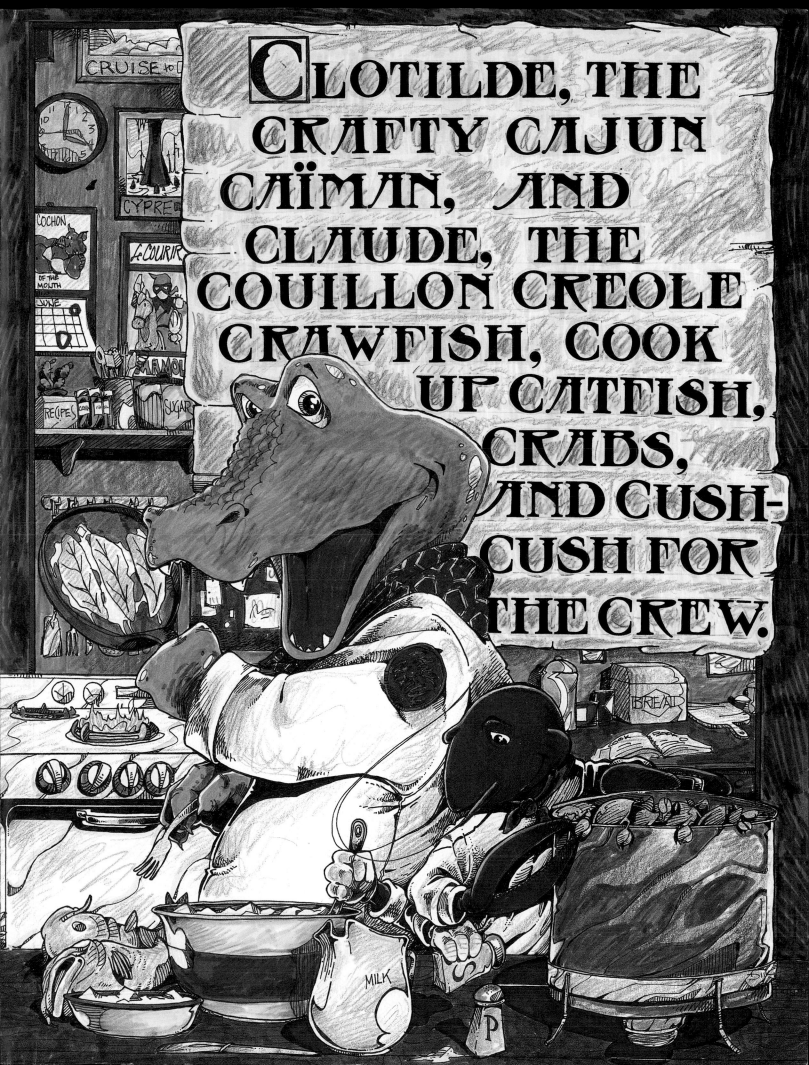

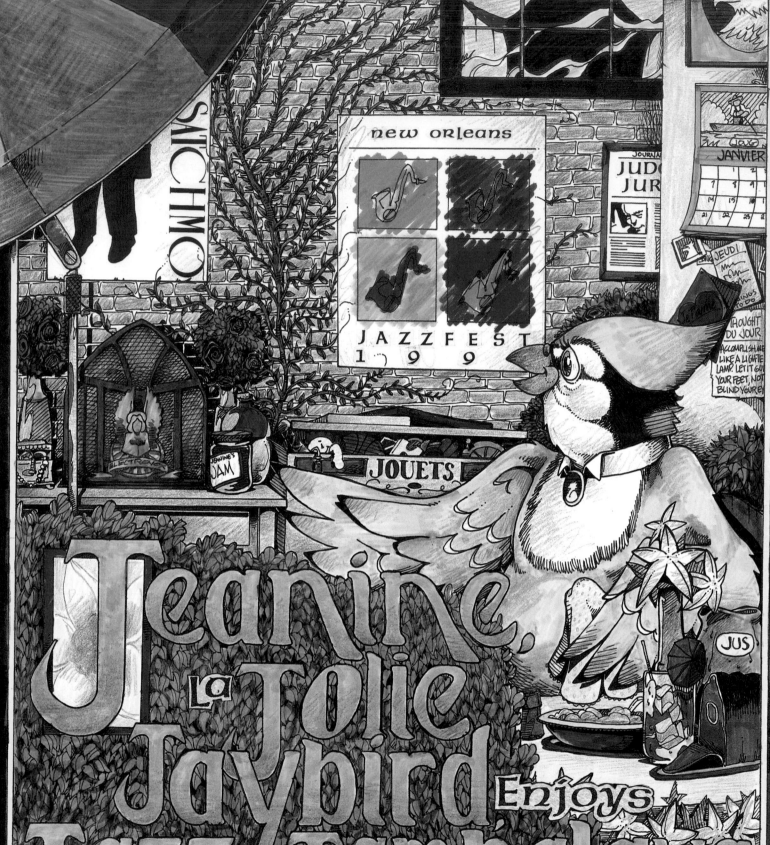

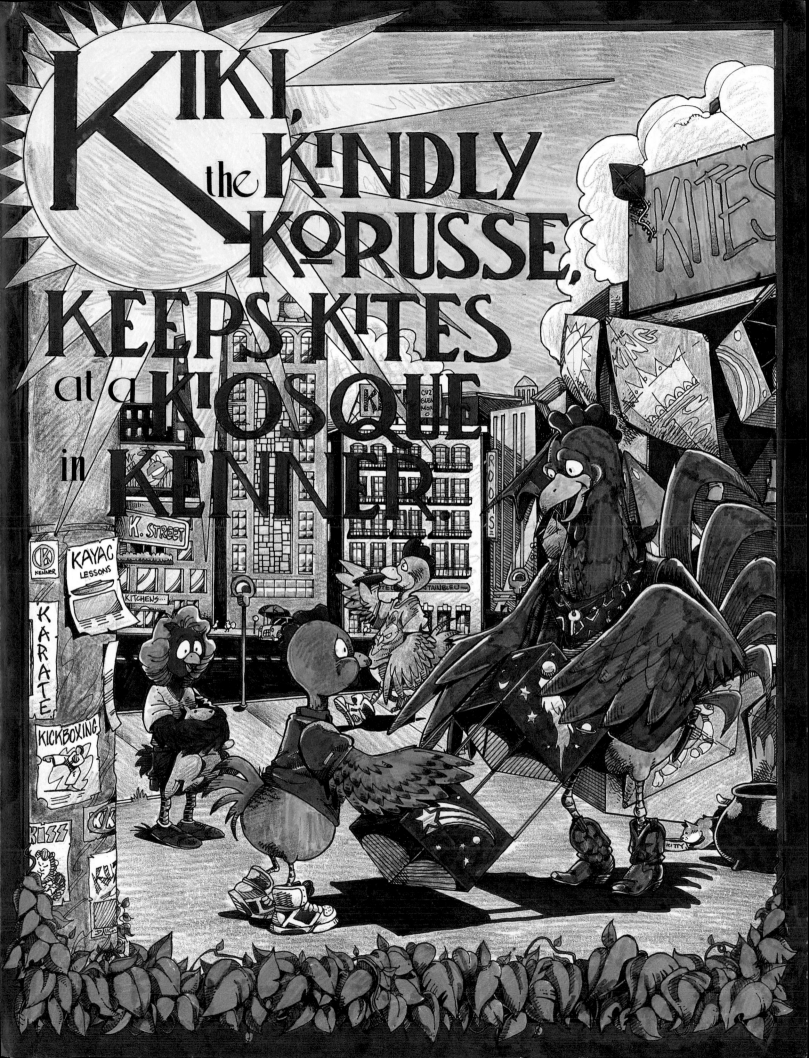

LAND OF LOVE, LAGNIAPPE, AND LAISSEZ LES BONS TEMPS ROULER!
LSU
BATON ROUGE
NEW ORLEANS
LA LIMONADE
.25¢ A CUP
BEWARE THE LOUP GAROU

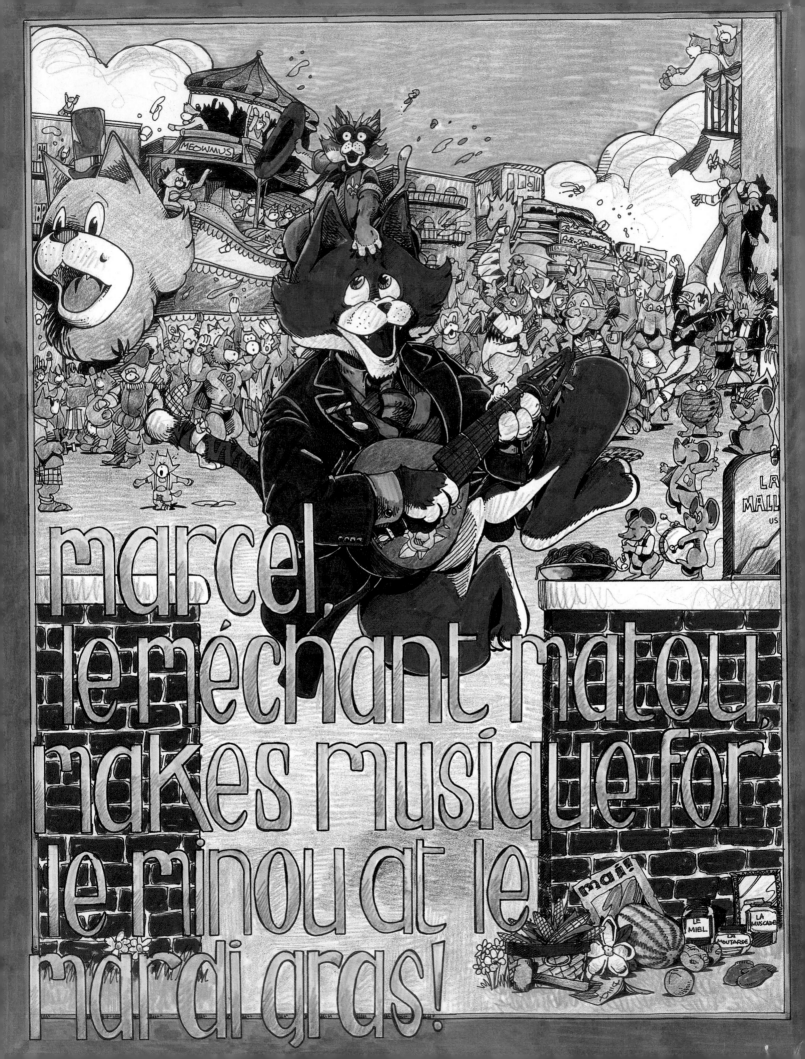

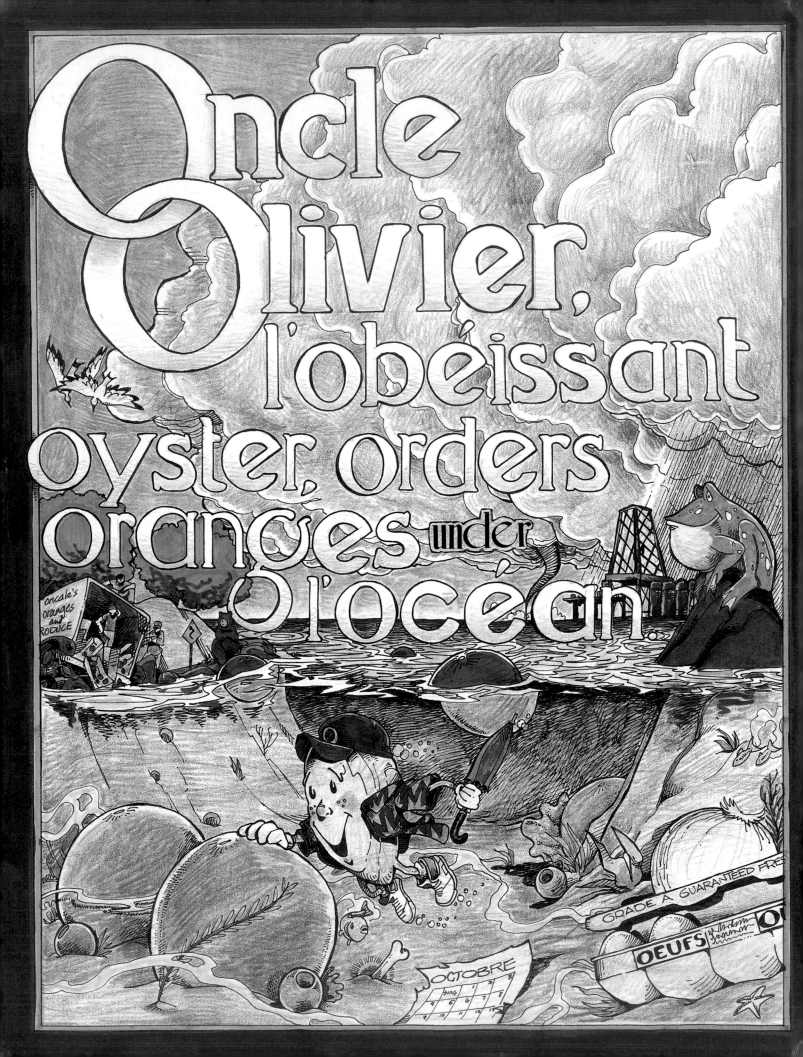

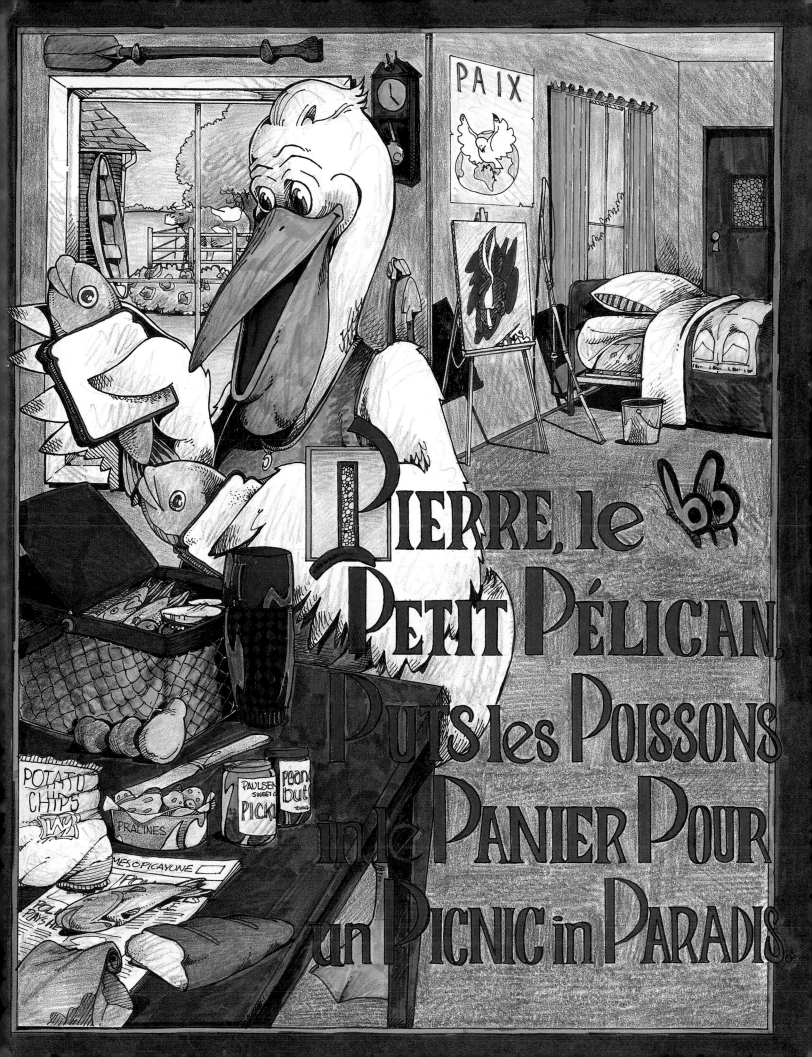

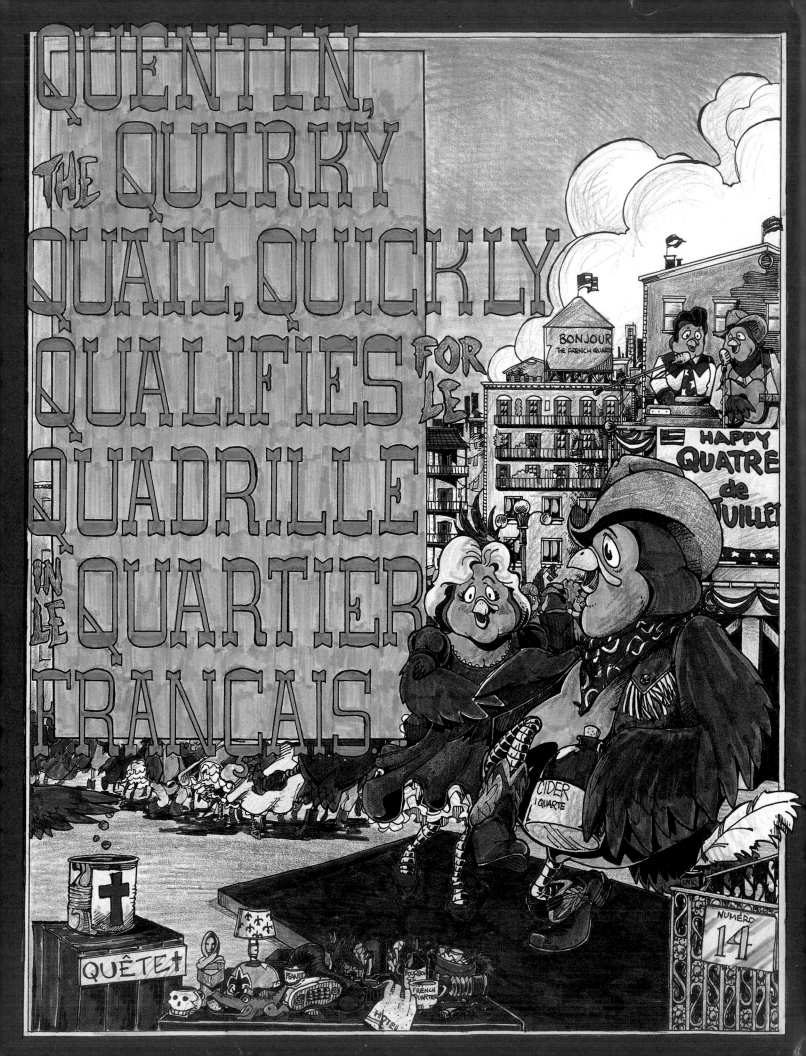

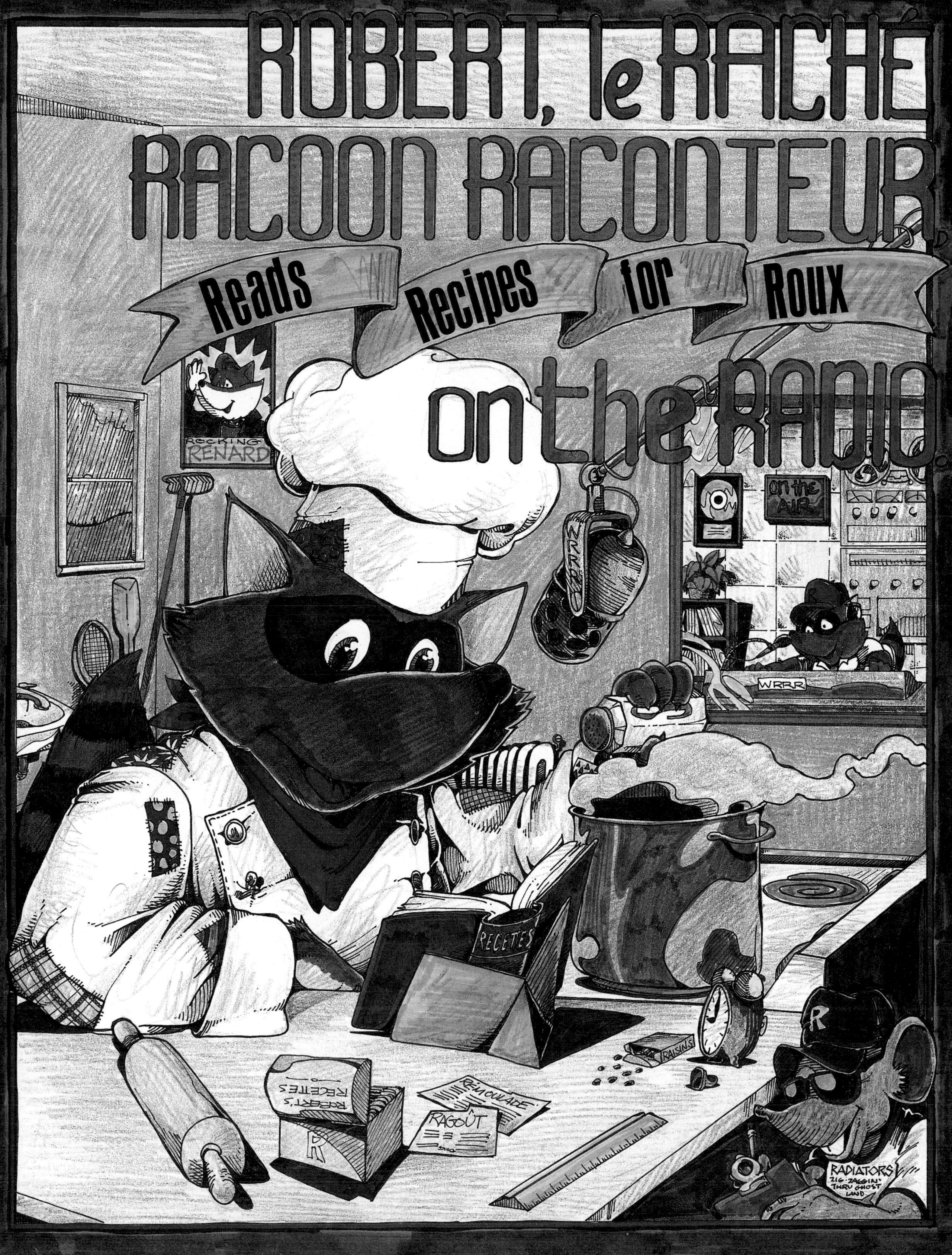
ROBERT, le RACHÉ
RACOON RACONTEUR
Reads Recipes for Roux
on the RADIO
ROCKING RENARD
WRRR
on the AIR
WRRR
RECETES
ROBERT'S RECETES
RÉMOULADE
RAGOÛT
RAISINS
RADIATORS
216 · ZAGGIN' THRU GHOST LAND

TOULOUSE, le TARDY TIGRE, TALKS TO TANTE THÉRÈSE by TÉLÉPHONE in THIBODAUX.
LSU TIGER
TULANE!!!!
TOUSSAINT
feast of all saints
LSU
TABAC
TABASCO

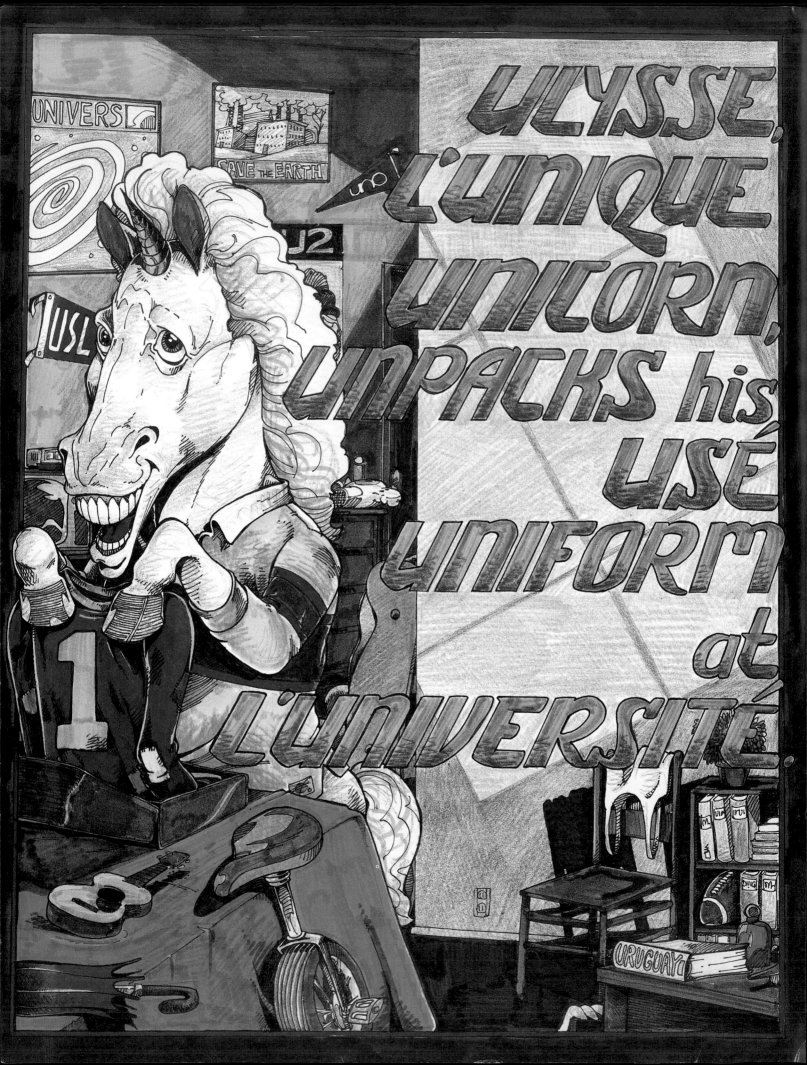

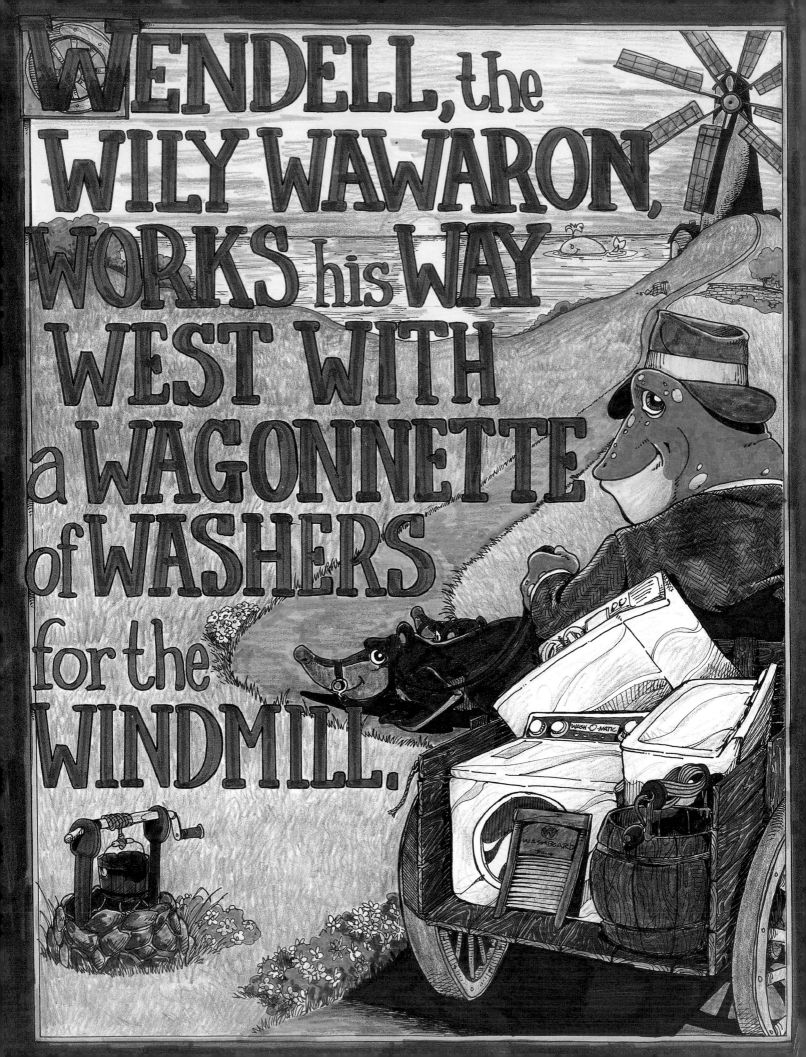

Xavier, l'eXtraordinaire eXpert, eXcuses the eXpenses of l'eXtravagant eXpériment.

GLOSSARY

amour (ah-MOOR): love
au nord (oh nor): northward
au sud (oh soo): southward
avec (ah-VEC): with

bayou (BYE-yoo): little river
beaucoup (bo-COO): a great many; a lot
bien habillé (byen ah-bee-YAY): well-dressed
bousillage (boo-see-AHZH): a mixture of mud and Spanish moss used as mortar during Louisiana's colonial days

caïman (cah-ee-MON): alligator
couillon (coo-YON): foolish; silly
créole (cray-OLE): literally "from the colony"; refers to anyone or anything from South Louisiana
cush-cush (CUSH-cush): Cajun dish made from milk and corn bread

dansante (don-SONT): dancing

egret (EE-gret): a large aquatic bird of the heron family
élégant (ay-lay-GON): elegant
étouffée (ay-too-FAY): Cajun dish cooked over high heat, then simmered or smothered
expériment (ex-pay-ree-MON): experiment
extraordinaire (ex-tror-dee-NAIR): extraordinary
extravagant (ex-trah-vah-GAHN): extravagant; fancy or expensive

fais do-do (fay DOH-DOH): a Cajun dance
filé (FEE-lay): powdered sassafras used as seasoning
fricassée (freec-ah-SAY): a Cajun stew
fromage (fro-MAHZH): cheese

gardesoleils (gard-so-LAY): sunbonnets
gris-gris (GREE-gree): voodoo spell or charm

habillé (ah-bee-YAY): dressed
haricots (hah-dee-CO): snap beans
héron (hay-RON): heron
hibou (hee-BOO): owl
honteux (hon-TUH): embarrassed
huîtres (WEET-ruh): oysters

Iberville (I-bur-vil): French explorer known as the "founder of Louisiana"

île (eel): island

Indiens (an-DYEN): Indians

Istrouma (is-TROO-muh): Indian word meaning "red stick"; refers to site of what is now Baton Rouge

jambalaya (jam-bah-LYE-uh): Cajun dish made of meat, sausage, or seafood mixed with rice

jambon (zham-BON): ham

jardin (zhar-DAN): garden

jolie (zho-LEE): pretty

kiosque (KEE-osk): small light structure with one or more open sides

korusse (ko-ROOS): rooster

lagniappe (LAN-yap): a little something extra; free

laissez les bons temps rouler (LESS-ay lay bon ton roo-LAY): let the good times roll!

Mardi Gras (MAR-dee grah): literally "Fat Tuesday"; Catholic celebration before Lent and the biggest free party in the world

matou (mah-TOO): tomcat

méchant (may-SHAHN): naughty

minou (mee-NOO): kittycat

musique (moo-ZEEK): music

naviguent (nah-VEEG): navigate

nerveux (nur-VUH): nervous

nord (nor): north

obéissant (oh-bay-ee-SAHN): obedient

océan (oh-say-AHN): ocean

oncle (ON-cluh): uncle

panier (pahn-YAY): basket

pélican (pay-lee-CAHN): state bird of Louisiana

petit (puh-TEE): small; tiny

poissons (pwah-SON): fish

quadrille (ka-DREE): square dance

Quartier Français (kart-YAY fron-SAY): French Quarter

raché (rah-SHAY): wretched

raconteur (rah-con-TUR): storyteller

roux (roo): flour-browned gravy used in making gumbo, etc.

samedi (SOM-dee): Saturday

sassafras (SAS-uh-fras): herb used in making filé

saucisses (so-SEES): sausages

Septembre (sep-TOM-bruh): September

sombre (SOM-bruh): somber

sucre (SOO-cruh): sugar

sud (soo): south

tante (tont): aunt

téléphone (tay-lay-FONE): telephone

tigre (TEEG-ruh): tiger

unique (oo-NEEK): unusual; special

université (oo-nee-ver-see-TAY): university

usé (oo-ZAY): worn-out

vanteur (von-TUR): boaster; braggart

Vermilionville (ver-MILL-yun-vil): original name of Lafayette

vexes (VEX-es): charms or curses

voodoo (VOO-doo): magical practice which began in Haiti

wagonnette (wa-gon-ET): small wagon or cart

wawaron or ouaouaron (wah-wah-RON): bullfrog

yacht (yaht): a light boat used for racing or pleasure

yam (yam): sweet potato

Yankie (YANK-ee): any American who does not speak French

yaourt (yah-OOR): yogurt

zombies (ZOM-beez): living dead brought back by voodoo

Zulu (ZOO-loo): one of the krewes of Mardi Gras, well known for their use of coconuts as "throws"; the Zulu king is the ruler over all Zulu Mardi Gras activities

zydeco (ZYE-deh-co): from "haricot," meaning snap bean; refers to a traditional style of Cajun music